TIMES OF LIFE

TIMES OF LIFE

Prayers and Poems

HUUB OOSTERHUIS

Translated by N.D. Smith

PAULIST PRESS
New York/Ramsey/Toronto

Originally published in Dutch under the titles *Hoever is de nacht* and *Dan zal ik leven*. This authorized translated selection has been composed of songs and prayers published or to be published by Ambo BV, Baarn (The Netherlands): © 1974, 1976, 1979.

Foreign rights consultant: James M. Boumans, B.A., M. Div., Utrecht (The Netherlands).

Library of Congress
Catalog Card Number: 79-89653

ISBN: 0-8091-2245-6

Published by Paulist Press
Editorial Office: 1865 Broadway, New York, N.Y. 10023
Business Office: 545 Island Road, Ramsey, N.J. 07446

Printed and bound in the
United States of America

CONTENTS

TIMES OF LIFE

AS LIGHT AS HE

AGAINST DEATH

TIMES OF LIFE

VISION

Then I saw
that the fourth seal had been broken.
And I heard a voice
calling with the sound of thunder: Come.
Before my eyes a horse loomed up,
ashen grey.
And its rider was death
and the abyss followed him.
And power was given to these two
over three-quarters of the earth.

Then I saw
that the fifth seal had been broken.
I saw the souls of all who had been slaughtered
and heard shouting: how much longer?

Then I saw
that the sixth seal had been broken.
Then the earth trembled and shook
like a woman in labor.
And the sun became as black as sackcloth
and the moon like blood
and the stars fell on the earth
like unripe fruit
pulled from the tree by the storm.
And the firmament was rolled up
like a scroll that has been read.
Islands and mountains were torn
away from their fixed spot.
All the great men of the earth and their followers,
authorities, property-owners, tyrants
and all men, slaves and free,
crept away into caves
and called to the rocks:
fall down on us,
for the day has come—
who can survive it?

Then I saw
him break the seventh seal.
And it became silent in heaven.

I saw a beast emerge from the sea.
It had ten horns and seven heads.
It wore royal crowns
and on its forehead was written
names dishonoring man.

Then the whole world full of admiration
followed the beast
and they began to worship the beast
because, they said,
who is as powerful as the beast?

So power was given
to the beast.

May all who understand
fathom the power of the beast.
The beast is people.

*Fragments from the book of Revelation
the vision of John freely adapted*

FOR FUTURE

That cobalt, lead and mercury
are no longer there
that there will be
no seagull
but men will starve
and be murdered

and parched and shrivelled
the fingertips the eyelids
of the soul

a child knows that.

Make the sun stand still
make time stand still
let it stay
as it is.

I need no future
if you are
not my future.

HOUSE FULL OF PEOPLE

This house full of people—
do you know who they are?
I would hope so.

Have you counted us,
do you know us by name?
You are the only one then.

1.
All living souls
conceivable and inconceivable
I commend to you.
You have after all made yourself available.
We may always call on you,
you have said:
I shall be there.

Do you already hear us
before we call on you?
Do you see beyond our faces
into our dark divided souls
to where we ourselves do not know
who we are?

We are bitter
because of our lost chances,
at our wits' end
because of happiness lost:
friendship broken
promises denied
a heart steeled.

We are despair
because of this world.

2.
What no eye has seen
no ear has ventured to hear,
what our fathers did not
dare to dream, we have
become: this world.

The dead unburied.
One desert your city.
Hunted, sacrificed,
slaughtered like game
your beloved people.

We are driven on
by storms of violence.
We are fastened
to millstones, like
damned souls: this world.

3.
You who have said:
comfort, my people—
for those who, lonely,
are pulled down
there is no comfort,
no saving word.

Are you the friend
who will raise them up?

For those who have
nothing but unhappiness,
people who want death—
for them you have words.

Where are you yourself?

4.
If you can speak,
then you can hear.

Hear all who call for peace
as for a happiness that cannot exist.

Hear the blood
that calls from the earth
that is shed in vain.

Hear those who are speechless,
mute, tortured,
everywhere in the world.

And all
who have no share in life
and cannot even count their dead,
because there are so many.

And the children of the spring in Prague,
the defeated. And the Jews.
And the sons of the Palestinians.

5.
Come what may come,
more intolerable
days of anxious
questioning: how further,
nights of no longer
knowing: who am I

come what may come,
but let it be for you
that we persist

and not for no one

that we drink the cup
to the last dregs,
that we live this life
until we die.

6.
The dead
who have perished in the earth
and who are scattered in the wind
and can never be found

those stolen from their homes
the incomplete ones
all who have gone away
without a greeting

what has he done with them—
he who never abandons
the work of his hands?

Place them as a seal
on your heart
as a seal on your arm

for love
is as strong as death.

7.
Guard the love of those who love each other.
You know how fragile, almost nothing,
two people are
and that their hearts are restless,
inconstant like the weather.
You have turned them
towards each other
so that they will not be half-people,
undirected, unfulfilled—
teach them to understand the deadly secret
that love means suffering,
that giving makes one live.
Give them time
to know and comfort one another.
Fan their passion,
give them patience
and infinite love,
so that they get through the night
with each other.

8.
Those who seek what is lost,
who are with the oppressed,
who with heart and soul
and all their understanding
try to soften
the worst suffering—
they reveal you,
they are yours.

Those who do not run away
from others in their misery,
who with their courage are
a counterbalance to the despairing,
who unseen and patient
languish, watch and pray,
hoping against hope.

Those who are harassed on all sides
but not at their wits' end,
who are doomed to die
but from day to day
are born anew—
they are of your stock.

9.
The unreflecting, dull men,
those whose hard hearts cannot be softened
and who do not want to hear
of other men's misery,
those who do not know what they do—
be patient with them.

But those who murder others,
divide the earth and plunder it,
the great men of this world—
challenge them
to become the people
whom you have seen in them.

You who love your enemies.

10.
Whom you have counted
whom you know by name
—and you are the only one

whom you have called
to be the soul
of this world
—but not one of us
knows why we

who call you:

may our song, our heart
not fall silent

may the eye of our soul
not become clouded

may the love of all for all
grow among us.

11.
You who wait on no one's glances,
cannot be bribed by sacrifice or money
and are not deceived by any song,
but see us as we are—

who order and beseech us
to be yours, your likeness, your son,
your right hand that does what must be done,
who order and beseech us
to give bread and clothing to the stranger—

who hope that we with faces unconcealed
reflect your light,
who bevel us into mirrors
in which your future can be seen—

you who looked for us
when we were not looking for you,
who ovecome your aversion every day,
tame your anger, cast off your pride,
bend your heart to compassion,
turn towards us—

you who catch us with your eyes
you who ask us:
who are you? do you want to?
come then.

12.
Your light breaks through
into us sometimes
irresistably

as when a child
is born.

Remember man
who is named
your child your kingdom
your light.

No darkness has ever
overpowered him.

Remember us
who were born like him
once and for good

who from his mouth
have heard your name,

who have to live
in the shadow of death

following him.

13.
You who in the beginning
called:
light
and the darkness fled,
day
and the night contracted,
people
and from what could not exist
we became people

you who have given meaning
to our existence,
you who have warmed our hearts

take us back
to the oasis of your will,
make your intention safe

found anew
this house full of people,
this earth.

May your name:
"I will be there"
direct us to peace.

TO BECOME A MAN AMONG MEN

Who like all his fellowmen
was called by his own name
when he was born far from here
and in a distant past

who was named Yeshua, Jesus
son of Joseph, son of David
son of Jesse, son of Judah
son of Jacob, son of Abram
son of Adam, son of man

who was called the son of God,
savior, vision of peace
light of the world, way to life
living bread and the true vine

who was loved, misunderstood,
was preserved in sign and language
as a very ancient secret
as a watchword handed down
as strange familiar story

who has become a name for me
in my memory, my truth
a voice in my conscience—
I remember him and name him,
as one dead who is not dead
as a loved one who is living

who chose to live
for the poorest of the poor
helper, traveling companion
brother of the least of men

who, when he went around
through the villages of his district
attracted and inspired people
reconciled them with each other

who was not above men, rigid
unapproachable, not a ruler
but lived like a servant

who gave up his life for his friends
who was betrayed by a friend
who was tortured on the cross
but prayed for his enemy
who, abandoned by God and man,
died like a slave

who was scattered on the field
like the smallest of all seeds
who throughout the winter waits
in the silence of death
who as corn will be gathered
who as bread will be shared
to become a man among men

who, hidden in his God,
has become our peace,
our soul that has come to rest
who greets us from his distance
who looks at us from nearby
like a child, a friend, another

I am mindful of him here, I name him
and commend him to you
as your loved one who is living
as the man who is near to you.

GRANT US THAT DREAM

O God, eternally unseen
our dear lord.

If right and peace are names for you,
how many times is your name
not cursed, denied,
here and everywhere on earth?

If in heaven and on earth
there is no other image of you
than a man, us people,
how many times
is your image not mocked
and smashed to pieces everywhere?

Eternally unseen
our dear lord.

If this war were the last
to be waged on earth,
the bitter end of all violence,
we would live again,
however disenchanted,
and would dare to believe
that your promise, your future
is not a chimera.

Grant us a day, an hour
to hope, against the facts
that peace is not unthinkable,
not impossible.

Grant us today, this hour,
in the midst of all the facts of weapons
and violence in war
the vision of peace.

If we pronounce the name of him
who was called your son
your messenger of peace, Jesus of Nazareth,

if we remember that he has gone
the only way that leads to peace,
that he has given himself,
broken, shared out,
as bread for every man,

grant that we may believe
that he
is not a chimera, a lie,
that he is the peace that we expect—
grant us that dream of a man.

O God, eternally unseen
our dear lord.

If we are told that peace is dawning,
do not let this be a lie,
political trickery,
short-term happiness, hope in vain—
let it last.

For the sake of so many million dead,
for the sake of all the human beings
who will come after us—
let it last.

THEN I WILL LIVE

It will be very early
as it was then.

The stone was rolled away.
I have got up from the ground.
My eyes can bear the light.
I walk and do not stumble.
I speak and understand myself.
People come towards me—
we are transformed and know each other

The morning mist rises.
I think I can see a barren plain.
I see full sheaves, long stalks, ears
in which the corn is swelling.
Trees surround the farmland.
Hills wave into the distance,
uphill, and become clouds.

Behind them,
crystal, blinding,
the sea that gave back its dead.

THE WAY OF A MAN

A hymn about Jesus

Born and brought up a man,
made to be the image
of him who lives and is love
who was and is and will be:
lord of the world,
all his brothers' keeper,

he did not desire power,
or status as a god,
and did not
submit
to the form of this world.

Did not, graspingly,
live for himself,
but got rid of his possessions,
stripped himself
gave himself away

and went the way
that leads along the seamy side
into the dark

and did not
turn around halfway
but went the whole way.

Stood in the slave market
to be sold
as the least of men
for an absurd price.

And thus became one of those
who are not worthy of man,
became all men
who are shamefully bartered

became no one
with whom no one is

became a leper

and those who see him
turn away from him.

And put on suffering
and wore it as a lamb

and let himself be struck
for others,
and be weighed down
with trouble and shame
so that many
might be free.

And was slaughtered
and was silent
in front of his shearers,
and was hanged
like a slave.

He became man,
a just man,
and his name was:
Slave Jesus child of man
image and likeness of him
who lives and is love,
equal to him.

May anyone who
looks at him
bend his heart
and recognize
that in hell and heaven
and on earth
no one deserves
the name of man
but he—

may only the one
who gives his life
to all men
receive that name
and live
like him.

We name him:
friend God
the first and the last.
You will name him:
our dear lord.

According to: Philippians 2:6-12,
John 13, Isaiah 53

WHO ALONE IS GOD

I bend my knees, my head,
I bend my heart
to him who is our father,
our inventor, our lover
our maker—

to whom all men
must turn, from whom
all men must drink:
all who want to be
father, source, beginning
in this world—

all who want to be
compassionate,
communicative, good.

Because he is the one
if he will/may
give us:

a soul that is indestructible,
an inside of living breath,
germs of traditional strength—

and may the future-man
live in our heart,
the son of man,
the morning star,
Jesus messiah.

May we be constant
and reliable,
rooted in love,
substructured with love.

If we were able
to understand,
with all the others
everywhere in the world
who have been
touched by him
how long and how broad love is,
how high love reaches,
how deep its abyss is.

If we could only be aware
who he is
who transcends our awareness:
the future-man

then we would be
filled with God,

who acts like yeast in us,
who inspires our soul,
who can make
unimaginably more of us
than we can think,
inexistably more
than we can expect
or even ask:

who alone is God
the rock that bears us
the light that shines through us
the air in which we breathe.

A text of Paul freely adapted

FOR STRENGTH

People curious astonished
behind barred eyes
splendid people
who bite off from themselves
laughing and crying.

People mild communicative
tired of war.

The man and the woman
who call:
who will receive me
where can I get rid of myself?

People as people—
others will never
exist. Will
another earth
even appear?

People, struck down
who do not strike back

who put to the test
do not hate the light

they are
as full of strength
as the rising sun.

BLESSED

Blessed is the invisible one
blessed the hidden one
blessed the living one
greeted love that gives thirst
light that gives sight.

Blessed people who are good
the hand that does not strike
the mouth that does not betray
the friend who does not deny
his friend.

Blessed are the merciful
and those who are open and lovable
and with whom it is good to associate.
Blessed are those who keep each other,
comfort, help and put up with each other.

Blessed is the woman for the man
and the man for the woman
and old for young
and strong for weak.

Blessed who knows
what is right and what is bad
and chooses accurately
and does not give way to any power
and does not fear any man.

Blessed is he who speaks
and loves without restraint
everything that lives.

Blessed is the new man,
past death,
who speaks in us,
who sighs and groans in us,
who lives in us.

Jesus messiah.

Who has given himself
lets himself be taken,
who is broken,
shared out from hand to hand,
is eaten as bread.

Blessed you, who small or great,
blind, fearful, groping, almost,
does as he. Blessed you
who, unseen and unknown,
does as he.

Blessed who,
purified by fear,
past death,
live in the light,
born again.

Blessed is the invisible one
blessed the hidden one
blessed the living one
greeted love that gives thirst
light that gives sight.

NEW NAME

Bearer of the unnameable name,
eternal, only, first and last,
love, knower of hearts,
hearer of unhearable crying,
seer of immeasurable suffering,
knowing and sympathizing with all

passionately wanting nothing more
than living people
eyes giving light
hearts with their husks removed

who his will
everything in everyone

who above lord and master
and power
chooses to be
the servant who toils for us,
the beast of burden carrying us,
the Chile lamb,
the black African,
who are slaughtered
in our place,
the least of men, God again
God once and for all

that is how you are
and still inexplicably more
or you are nothing and no one.

Bearer of unnameable names
eternal here-and-now
unexpectedly arising
always suddenly present on time
distant friend

no one, born of men,
you became nameless, were nowhere,
could never be found for you

people who could no longer exist,
stripped, dispossessed,
exist for you

we, I, all men,
cattle for slaughter, dogs,
sold, crushed,
living dead,
dead and buried,
exist for you

and nothing is nothing for you

and no one—anyone—
became no one for you

that is how you are

and past all these words
inexpressibly more
or you are nothing and no one.

GREAT AND EXALTED

My soul is as young
as on the day it was created—
it is even much younger.
I tell you, I would be ashamed
if tomorrow
it was not younger than it is today.

I have a strength in my soul
that is quite open to God.
I am as sure of that as I am of my life.

When he created the soul
he put his hands into himself
and made the soul according to his image.
He is the soul of the soul.

Whoever is at home in all places
is dared on God.
And whoever throughout all ages
becomes one and himself—
for him God is here and now.
In whomever everything that is created
becomes silent,
in him God bears his son.

We should not be silent
about great and exalted things—
our words should be great and exalted.

Eckehart, 13th century, freely translated

WITH YOU

With you nothing dies.
In you all things
become alive.

You never go away
you are always near.

No one knows who you are
but I do know a little:
what you are not.

The joy of the angels
and the blessed
is but a spark
compared with your joy—
you laugh and laugh
for you are glad
about all the good
that is done.

I am sad
and not yet born

I am not a match for you.

FOR BIRTH

Break the membranes.
Draw us out. Tie
our navel cord.
Open us.

Let us flow
full of living breath
and cry
born at last.

Let us flow
full of living breath
and laugh
born at last.

Let us flow
full of living breath
and know
born at last.

PSALM

Do you know me? Whom do you know, then?
Do you know me better than I do?

Eyes that look through the sun,
seeking the spot where I live,
you are—
picture-language for someone
who is nice and unmeasurably fair,
who neither stands nor falls nor feels
as I do, is not cold and haughty.

Here is the spot where I live:
a chair on the water, a window
which the weather, clearing up,
or the dusk, falling, passes.
Did you call? Here I am.

I do not know what is in me,
how much, how little, I say
the words that I have learnt
as well as possible: "love,
yes, I shall, I want to, you,
we, I, people"—but what is genuine,
undeniable and purified
in these words. Do you know?

I should like to speak one word,
that is true and is mine,
that bears who I am, that holds
and stands erect
like a man looking at me
and saying:
I am your purest self,
do not fear, understand me, I am.

It never crosses my lips.
But you have already understood it.
Are you, then, deeper silence
than my speechlessness in me,
are you so selflessly present in me
that you hear the sighing and groaning
that I cannot hear myself?

Do you hear being born in me
the other person I would like to be?

Are you the only one from whose eyes
my nakedness is not concealed?
Can you bear it, as no one else can,
that I have no light, am not warm,
that I am not beautiful, not much,
that no spring arises
in my depths,
that I only have this face,
no other?
Am I seen, taken
by you, shamelessly,
by no one less?
Is that not much too much
true?

Do you know me? Whom do you know then?
Do you know me better than I do?

I HARDLY KNEW YOUR NAME

Clock stopped. Door of thoughts
closed behind me.
Above the abyss a singing bridge descends.
Deciphered I turn back
to the gentlest spot in my memory:
your name.

I hardly knew your name
when you asked me.

Since you have asked me
who I am and why
I can no longer exist
apart from you.

You, inexpressible,
god-of-people is your name.
Voice calling me: who are you
is your name.
Voice calling me: where is your brother
is your name.

I hardly knew your name
when you asked me.

Name that is no name
may you live and prosper—
may this house be full of your voice
may our soul be full of your voice
our body light of your light
your name the way that we go.

May your son, your servant
be the way that we go
may Jesus of Nazareth
be the way that we go.

His word, his spirit,
his way to life:
the way that we go.

He who took this bread
and shared it out,
he who shared his life
until death,
he is the way
that we must go.

He who took the cup
he who shared his soul and
his blood and his life's strength
and gave them up,
he is the way
that we must go.

He is your way
your name is no name
he is our future
he is your name.

I hardly knew your name
when you asked me.

Since you have asked me
who I am and why
I can no longer exist
apart from you.

If I had not yet been born
I would like to be born,
if I had not yet been made
I would like to be made
by you.

If I had never
heard your name,
would you call me
would you seek me
would you give me
food and drink?

Would you share
your life with me
like this bread?

Clock stopped. Door of thoughts
closed behind me.
Above the abyss a singing bridge descends
Deciphered I turn back
to the gentlest spot in my memory:
your name.

I hardly knew your name
when you asked me.

A psalm, a table prayer
for the celebration of the Eucharist

DEEPEST ABYSS

Deepest abyss, highest
height, into you I take flight
restlessly happy.

When you beckon
the storm wind kneels.

My most undeniable
dearest.

Ever begun flowering
fire ineradicable.

Gushing cold spring-water
overflowing the tired
midday of my soul.

FOR ANSWER

I will not hold my tongue to you
—why should I?
My heart is restless, sad
rebellious scornful in me.

Who are you that I should find you important
that I should think of you every day
that I should measure myself against you?

Turn your eyes at last away away
from him, they say to me
—but then I have no answer.

I never have nothing with you.

Against almost better judgment
I place my hope in you.
My fate is to wait
the whole of my life for you.

Living with a dead, invisible
loved one, self-invented—
why should I
not give you up?

But I can do nothing else
but call: love me.

NIGHT PRAYER

You are above the sea.
You are silver pole star.

We sail by you.

I was glad when men told me:
we sail by him.

Eternal flame of peace
kindle in us your peace.

High watchful, you are
silence, night of eternity
to eternity.

FOR LIGHT

Friendly light
gentle light
sweet light.

Unpayable
you cannot be bought
in any alley
and on any beach
and from any queen.

Short-lived light—
you last for a day
then you go out.

But in you I live
the coming going
evaporating hours,
the restlessness of love
the certainly uncertain
minutes of love.

Light that nourishes me
unnoticeably
that bears me
unnoticeably as the sea.

Dead still hazy light
thoughtful light.

Descend on this city
and rain on the tense
diffident faces,
hurried vague
chilled faces
of people.

Dear light.

Voice from heaven
that says
that we may be
now, who we are.

Inescapable light
blind making light.

Pseudonym for him
who lives eternally.

Light light.

Love that moves
the sun and all stars.

FOR WATER

May all the rainwater of the future
wash me clean.
May all the showers of the coming century
rinse me.
May, one day,
one waterfall after another
come down on my head.
All the supplied that you, heaven,
have stored in your compassion
for steppe and desert:
give them to me.
May also the waves of the sea
break over me
and its surf beat against me.
May the whirlwind rise
and tear from me floor and roof
and everything that I have
gathered around me.
Let it blow away
all the gold-dust and rust
under which I am buried.
Then may he come to me
he who strikes the springs
who can find
all the water in the world.
Let him make me
a spring that flows gently and gaily.

May I give myself
to the roots of the grass
and the flowers.

WHO BORE ME

Who bore me
on eagle's wings

who launched me
into space
and when I fell screaming
caught me
with your pinions
and threw me up again

until I could fly
by my own efforts.

WHO DID NOT DRAG ME

Who did not drag me,
did not push, but beckoned
over your threshold

who did not tear the veil
of my fear, but lifted

who with only
your voice made me so tender
that I wanted.

WHEN YOU CALLED ME

I hardly knew your name
when you called me.

Since you ask me
where I am, I am struck dumb
and want to hide—
if I appear
I look into the light
of your hidden face.

I hardly knew your name
when you called me.

Other gods their names are mountains
flowers—sowed, islands like dreams
primordial forest—covered, palaces of eyes,
speaking serpents, thrones,
a mother-of-pearl beach.

Your name is fallow land,
the brackish soils
of yesterday and now,
the haze of germinating morning.
Your name is stammering mouths,
springs hidden,
words that do not exist.
Your name is people bent
under a heaven of dark and light
raising each other up, sometimes.

Your name is the hand
that strikes me
makes me shout, makes me breathe,
the shears that cut me loose,
the mouth that calls to me:
that I shall live.

I hardly knew your name
when you called me.

Since you ask me
where I am, I am struck dumb
and want to hide—
if I appear
I look into the light
of your hidden face.

I hardly knew your name
when you called me.

AS LIGHT AS HE

BLESSED YOU

1.
Blessed you
for your wisdom that is hidden
for your dream that you have cherished
from all eternity:
that we might one day become people
in the full light.

Blessed you
for what no eye has seen
no ear has heard—
but now it has also arisen in our hearts,
since you have spoken your word to us.
Your dream has become our conscience
and it will never again be silent in us
and it will never again be
as though we had not heard it.
Blessed are you
for making people responsible,
for making all men liable
for the future of all men.

Have you no other blessing
than this call
that is like a consuming fire?

Send another—
we cannot speak,
we are still children.

2.
Blessed you
who have called:
"man, where are you,
man, where is your brother?"—
did you give one man
to the other
for their children now to kill each other?
We are those children of men
and everything that happens, everywhere in the world,
is our world and our history
and all life that is destroyed
is our life—we ourselves are those
who kill and are killed.
Blessed are you.

3.
Blessed you
for people who hear your word
and do it—
they are like trees
planted by living water.

Blessed you
for all those who bear each other,
give comfort and light,
make life easier in secret.

Blessed are you
in those who go on your way,
who know and honor you,
doing justice,
who honor the stronger in their midst,
who do not mock the deaf man
or make the blind man stumble.

Blessed are you
for people who believe in peace and love
despite the power of the facts,
for those who endure
in this world,
uncrowned,
and do not hate the light.

Blessed are you for nameless people
who are ready to suffer
for the sake of your new earth.

Blessed are you for all who are foolish,
who do not hold their own, who do not want power,
who only hunger for your kingdom—
blessed are you.

4.
Blessed you
who have chosen
the foolishness and impotence of the world
to put all worldly wisdom, all powers to shame.

Blessed, incomprehensible God,
who has chosen
the least in the world, the despised,
what does not exist,
to refute what exists—
you who exposed the independent power of this world
as foolishness
when you gave us your least man, your own son,
that slave who was tortured to death, crucified,
as the messiah.

Blessed you
for your foolishness wiser than men,
for your impotence more powerful than men.

5.
Come into me, word that transcends me
as the sun in heaven,
as the wind that blows where it will;
come, word that must be said and given to me,
come as a nearest person on my way and look at me.

Speak in me, word that is in me,
deeper than I can see and feel,
word that wants to germinate in me like a seed,
that wants to rise up out of me as a new man;
word that will accompany me, light going ahead of me,
as long as it is night, as long as this world lasts.
Word that leads me
to the land promised to our fathers—
that will be a land of springs
and streams of living water,
a land full of bread, vineyards, honey and olives,
there the stones are of steel
and the mountains of copper,
there we shall live
and be satisfied.

MAKE US PEOPLE

1.
Reveal to us, you who are eternal,
your son, your messiah, Jesus of Nazareth,
who gave himself,
who broke our lack of grace,
who will set us free
from the tyranny of this world.
In him you have revealed
your whirling strength, your spirit
that makes us empty and receptive,
that makes everything full and loads with light.

2.
O our father in heaven—
you make your sun rise
on men bad and good,
you send your rain to all, right and wrong;
you tell us, through your son,
to be perfect and undivided of heart,
Make us undivided of heart,
make us people made whole, healed,
cheerful, firm and purposeful,
unshakably directed
towards your kingdom and its justice.
May we be perfect like you;
make us effective, brave, infectious,
make us indestructible, as you are.

3.
When your word, your light, your beloved
came into our life
our fate took a turn.
You did not spare us,
but misery became our portion,
scorn, temptations, doubt—
anyone who wants to live in your light
obviously has not much else to expect.
But the one who puts us to the test,
has not, for all his stirring up of trouble,
overpowered us, thanks to you.
We are still standing, keep us on our feet,
keep us sober and alert,
so that we are not taken by surprise,
like a thief, by your day.

4.
Fan into us
the spirit of your prophets.
Make us one community
with the first followers of your messiah.
We know exactly what we are asking:
that we shall be hated
as your prophets were once hated.
Make us do your word in such a way
that we have to suffer and be persecuted
for the sake of justice.

5.
May your word be firmly fixed in us.
Inflame us, so that we may say:
did our hearts not burn when he was speaking to us?
Make all sadness in us die.

God our peace,
make us holy through and through,
so that we may be kept sound
and unblemished in heart and soul for you
until the day
that will come
Jesus, the lord, the messiah.

SONG OF THE CALLED

God's word comes
freely and calls
the dead to life
people by name.
Watch and reply
courageously
when the lord
goes past
calling your houses.

The word called
Moses with power:
you must set free
the people I love.
The word seized
Jeremiah with power:
speak for me,
I place my words
in your mouth.

Flee abroad
over the sea,
Jonah, God will still
overtake you,
in the fish
he will catch you,
as a little
floundering fish
he catches you.

Jesus called:
Simon come!
No, lord, go away,
I am unworthy.
Great awe
had seized him.
Jesus said:
a fisher of men
I make you.

Son of God
show your faith
call us by name
make us willing.
At your word
we will embark
in your spirit
fishers of men
make us, lord.

SONG OF THE ENEMY

The liar from the beginning
that spirit of murder and fire
tries to torment and devour us—
O lord, bind your archenemy
with a strong hand.

O lord, make your community safe,
make us your kingdom.
An evil spirit has desecrated us,
a spirit of discord and doubt—
banish him, lord.

What you in love have joined together
he breaks apart again.
He sows confusion and destroys peace—
you suffered most from him
but resisted him.

If our sin is ever excessive
your grace is always there
in superabundance for all.
Jesus, redeem us from all evil
and from death.

Blessed the breast that fed you,
blessed the womb that bore you.
Blessed by God whoever is born
again and humbly hears your word
and keeps it.

A DOUBLE SONG

1.
Why when
from what layer of air,
from how deep a vacuum
did we become
so inexistable
inescapable I and you—
side and other side
word reply tide
and counter-tide?

This day today:
alienated re-owned
gone astray refound
who are we?
Love that can hardly
be lived, I and you.
Love is no word
for this fire
consuming now and here.

But some time, God knows
from what layer of earth,
from how deeply petrified
a mother's womb,
he will call us
and we shall stand new and bare
in morning light
unpreventably free
as light as he

2.
Why then
from what layer of air
from how deep a vacuum
did we become
so inexistable
inescapable I and thou—
side and other side
word reply tide
and counter-tide?

This day today:
alienated, re-owned
gone astray refound
who are we?
Life that can hardly
be kept, I and thou.
Life is thy word
for this fire
consuming now and here.

But some time, thou knowest
from what layer of earth,
from how deeply petrified
a mother's womb,
thou wilt call me—
I will stand beside thee
blazingly new and bare in light
unpreventably free
as new as thou.

SONG OF THE MISSING

1.

Those who are dumb, distant, cold, stone in stone,
those who cannot be found, lost in deadly desert:
who knows their name, what has he done with them
who is called you, unimaginable you,
who crying seeks and finds the lost child,
who digs life itself out of death?

2.

However dark this existence may be,
however black my grief, it is not despair,
because you who guide my life are God.
You are enough for me. You are my certainty.
The light of my eyes shines from your face.
The day will come when I may take my rest.

3.

Those who are ill-fated will be blessed.
Those who are rejected will be in you.
Those who have turned from you will find you.
Unloved, for no reason loved by you.
Laughter will be heard when your last word
brings splendor to this torn universe.

A SONG TO LIGHT

Light that strikes us in the morning
premature light in which we are
cold, one by one, and insecure,
light cover me, spur me on.
Let me not drop out, let none of us,
heavy and wretched as we are,
fall out of grace with each other
and be aimless and beyond reach.

Light, representative of my city,
persistent light that overcomes,
fatherly light, permanent shoulder,
bear me up, I am your child looking.
Light, child in me, look through my eyes
and see if somewhere a world is dawning
where men may live a worthy life
and bear their names in peace.

Everything will yield and be blown away
that is not grafted on to light.
Language will only sow destruction,
nothing remains of what we do.
Light, you many voices can be heard
as long as our hearts do not cease to beat.
Men love you, light, the firstborn
and last word of him who lives.

AN OLD STORY—OUR OWN MYSTERY

Three texts for the baptism of a child

1.
A drop of water and a few words,
the name of Jesus, the name of God.

That gesture, that sign
has a long history
and anyone who wants to understand
what it means
must listen to an old story.
It is, God knows,
our own story, our own mystery.

We are just a little group of slaves
—of course we are not,
but of course in a sense we are—
a little group of slaves,
tormented, badly treated,
cannot bear it any longer;
they wrench themselves away
from the establishment,
break out
of subjection
to divine laws
of master and servant,
of rich and poor
of this is the way things are
—all those principles according to which . . .
the whole system of it has always been like this
and it always will be—
people wrench themselves away
and fight to get loose.

They achieve the impossible
and break through fear,
despair and cynicism
and make a new beginning.

What they do is called "exodus."
What they do is believe.

Exodus.
It is risky, hard.
They go away,
through the sea, through the desert,
following a vision,
towards a land
where freedom is lord and master,
where there is a city of peace
and justice.

Centuries later.
The land has been reached,
the city has been built.
And everything is as it is:
established order, fixed opinions,
the law is law,
god is god,
dead is dead,
and what cannot be allowed
cannot be allowed.
And if you have grown to the size of an adult
you cannot go back into your mother's womb
and be born again.

There is a man
in that land, in that city,
who says:
if you are not born again
you will not see
the kingdom of God
—his power, his effect in this world.

He says:
with God everything is possible.
He says:
you are to forgive
seventy times seven.
He says:
blessed are those
who hunger and thirst
after justice.
He says:
do not be anxious about your life.
He says:
whoever among you wants to be the first
must become the servant of all.
He says:
I am the way, I am the life.

And what he does
is impossible.
("He blasphemes God"
is what they say about him.)
But poor people and slaves,
the rejected, the possessed,
those who are disparaged—
with him they feel set free.

And when he is dead,
cast out,
crucified as a slave,
he is recognized
and believed in.
A little group of people
make a new beginning.
Set free by him,
they go on exodus again
and are born again
although they are old
and wise and the size of adults.
They say:
he is the way,
he is the life.

Such people
are still among us.
What they do is believe.
Believe
that things can be different,
that slaves will be set free
and the blind will see
and the dead live
and the established order
will be turned upside down,
anxiety will be driven out
and men will no longer be possessed,
swords will be beaten into ploughshares
and armies disbanded.
People who believe
that the impossible is possible.
With God.

Such people
are still among us
everywhere and nowhere.

They are not "the" Church—
Catholic or Protestant.
But there are such people
in all the churches
and more and more
outside the churches.

Do they really exist?
Complete people? Firm?
Sure of themselves and their faith?
They are not very firm.
They are unsteady.
They sigh and groan
as in the pain of giving birth.
They are becoming.
They are always
born again.

How can a little child
understand such words?
It is your child
and will "understand," gradually,
what is being said here with such trouble,
because you have chosen
to take your child with you
on the way that you are going,
on the exodus,
following the one man.
Your child will be able to understand, perhaps,
as you yourselves understand more and more
what is meant.
You have chosen
to teach your child
and will be your child's first companions
on the journey.
Your living experience
will show them what it is

to be born
and to be born again and again,
seventy times seven.

A drop of water and a few words,
the name of Jesus, the name of God.
That gesture, that sign
has a long history
and anyone who wants to understand
what it means
must tell an old story again.

2.
A prayer
Child of people,
we pray that you will have
the fullness of God
a new heaven
the new earth,
that you will be
now and again and again
and all your life
filled to overflowing
with the hope
that can bring about what is not yet,
that you will live in the spirit of Jesus
and follow his way
to the world
that he beheld,
towards his God and father,
that you will be at home
in all his words of hope and future,
of faith and love,
that you will be strong
and fruitful, good and happy.

O God, you have as much blessing in you
as the sun and the rain:
bless the parents of this child,
so that they will find the strength and wisdom
to lead their child on the way of peace
to a land where justice is living.

Let them remain faithful to their child
and respect him/her wherever he/she may go.
Let them hold on to each other
on that long way.
Let them understand and love each other.
Let them look again and again and find.

Remember and bless
all those who are here in this circle,
all those who live in this district
and who with their evil and their good
make the world
in which this child of people
will grow up.

Our father, you who know us,
you who alone can fulfill us,
make us walk in the footsteps of your son,
Jesus of Nazareth,
who told us
that we have no future and no life
unless we become
like little children,
that we shall see your kingdom
if we are born again and again,

whose life was a living example of these words,
who gave all his possessions, all his love,
his heart and the strength of his spirit,
who followed
the way of sacrifice,
the way of life—
who on the night of his suffering and death
took bread
as a sign
and said:
I am here myself,
this is my body,
I want to be shared out
as bread and eaten—
who took the cup with wine
and handed it on
and said:
I am here myself,
drink me, I give
my blood and my life
for a new covenant of all people.

So we take this bread, this cup,
as a sign of our faith
that his way is reliable
and can be followed,
a way to life for our children.

3.
A song
He who wants us all to live on earth,
he has entered our own life.
He was baptized
so that he might endure our death and life.
Jesus was baptized in the Jordan.

Then he accepted the evil of the world,
servant of God who bears all suffering—
then the spirit
drove God's loved one into loneliness,
lamb of God who takes our death away.

Forty days he fasted in a foreign land,
consecrated lamb and servant by the spirit,
he was tempted
to accept a kingship of power and majesty,
he who had come to serve his fellowmen.

Who, baptized to live in his spirit,
is tempted to faithlessness and doubt,
you who hear
the enemy's voice whispering in your dreams,
Jesus will teach you to keep to God's word.

FOUR TEXTS FOR A POLITICAL
EVENING PRAYER

1.
Then he sent his prophet Nathan to us
with these words:
Two men lived
in the same city.
One was rich, the other poor.
The rich man had great flocks of sheep
and herds of cattle.
The poor man had nothing
except one little ewe-lamb
that he had bought and
that he had been able to keep alive.
She had grown up with him
and with his children.

She ate from his plate,
drank from his cup
and slept in his lap.
She became as precious to him
as his own daughter.
One day someone visited the rich man.
And the rich man had not the heart
to slaughter one of his own sheep or oxen
and make a meal of it
for the stranger
who was visiting him.
So he decided
to take the poor man's ewe-lamb
and have her slaughtered.
We called out in anger:
By God, the man who did that
deserves to die.
Then Nathan said to us:
You are that man.

2.

Then he sent his prophet Amos to us,
with these words:
I set up a lamentation over you.
You who trample on the weak,
seize and maltreat the innocent.

He who is and who will be says this:
I hate, I abhor your feasts,
I cannot bear your sacrifices,
spare me the sound of your songs,
I will not listen to your harps.
Do justice and righteousness.
Make justice flow,
unpreventable as a river.
Make righteousness flow
like living water.

You who contemplate
your murderous attack on the poor,
you who hatch plots
to kill the needy,
you say to yourself:
I will buy them for money,
the least of men,
for a pair of shoes,
the poor
—therefore the earth will shake
therefore the earth will become black
in the light of day.

He who is and who will be says this:
I will plunge your feasts into mourning,
your songs will become lamentations.
And the last day of your life
will be bitter.

3.
a. A song based on Psalm 24
The earth is the Lord's and those who live in it.
His are its depth and its future. He has
built it on the water and anchored it firmly.

Who may climb to its height? Who may
stand with uplifted head in his house?
People with righteous hands.

People with hearts that are not divided,
those who have turned from lies and appearance.
People uncrushable, laden with light,

who do the good that must be done,
the kind that asks and fights for him,
that wants to see him with their own eyes.

b.

Gates, lift up and raise your heads,
reach up higher, ancient doors.
Here comes the eternal, the radiant one.

Who is the eternal, the radiant one?
It is he who fights for righteousness.
It is the God of the poor, the strong one.

Gates, lift up and raise your heads,
that he may enter, the God of the poor,
the strong, the eternal, the radiant one.

Who is he, the strong, the radiant one?
He who made us and called us to righteousness,
our God, the eternal, the radiant one.

4.
Prayer of petition
Teach me. Open me. Be yeast in me.
Make me the heir
of psalms and prophetic visions.
Enlighten the eyes of our soul
and teach us how to pray.
Let us see how, with heart and mind,
we must deal with your plan for the future
that includes everyone and does justice to everyone,
your world that is to come.
Your will be done, your name be established:
a society in which no one
is humiliated, enslaved, scorned and abandoned.
Expose my reluctance, my cynicism.
Make us patient and wise,
so that we can encourage and help each other
to accept this change of life.
May the churches to which we belong
be places of learning for our consciences.

May no word be heard behind their façades
apart from your word
calling us to justice.
May no voice echo under their domes
apart from your voice
calling us to conversion.
May we not sleep but stay awake and watch
in the house of your name.
May we be purified in this furnace, this life,
so that we become people who are good.
May we grow until we become adult people
who will recognize you full of joy
as their friend and their father.

AGAINST DEATH

*The word that I give you today
is not too high for you.
It is not beyond your reach.
It is not in the sky,
so do not say:
"Who will get it for us from the sky?"
It is not beyond the seas,
so do not say:
"Who will get it for us from beyond the seas?"
My word is near.
It is in your mouth.
It is in your heart.
You can fulfill it.*

LIFE AND DEATH

Hear, Israel.
I set this before your eyes:
life and happiness,
but also death and destruction.
If you walk in the way of my word
you will live,
you and your children,
from generation to generation.

Hear, Israel.
What does the lord your God ask of you?
Only to love him and know him,
doing justice,
to walk in his way,
to be devoted to him,
heart and soul,
doing justice,
to keep his words
that he gives you today,
so that all will go well for you.
Circumcise your hearts, then,
and be stubborn no longer,
for the lord your God
is God above all gods and powers,
above all those in power
and all who do injustice.
He is great and powerful,
the only one who inspires awe.
He is no respecter of persons
and never accepts bribes.

He does justice to the orphan and the widow.
He loves the stranger.
He gives him bread and clothing.
Love the stranger in your midst, then,
for you yourselves were strangers
and slaves in a strange land.

Love your neighbor, who is as you.
You shall not covet your neighbor's wife
or his land or anything that is his.
You must not exact interest from your neighbor.
Once every seven years
you must grant him a remission of his debts.
There need be no poor in your midst.

When you harvest what has grown on your land,
do not reap to the very edge of your field
and do not glean what is left.
When you harvest your vineyard,
do not pick it over afterwards
or gather the grapes that have fallen.
Leave them for the poor and the strangers.
It is I. No other is your God.
You shall not steal.
Do not falsify my name.
Do not desecrate my name
or deprive it of its strength.
Do not mislead each other.
You shall not cheat your neighbor or dispossess him.
You shall not withhold the wages of the worker
who is hired by the day till the following morning.

If you have taken your neighbor's cloak as a pledge,
you must give it back to him at sunset,
because it is the only covering that he has
and how will he be able to sleep without it?

If you see one of your neighbor's sheep straying,
do not let it run away, but take it back to him.
If he lives a long way from you
or you do not know him,
take care of it and keep it with you
until he asks for it back.
You must do the same with his donkey,
his garment and anything that he loses.

You shall not mock a deaf man.
You shall not put a stumbling block
in the way of a blind man.
You must honor me. No other is your God.
You shall not be unjust in administering justice.
Do not favor the poor
or dance attendance on the rich.
You must judge your neighbor justly.
You must take no bribes,
and violate the law,
for bribes blind men's eyes and distort their words.
You must passionately pursue justice alone.

These words that I give you today—
impress them on your heart and soul,
write them on your doorposts and your tables,
write them on your forehead
and on the palm of your hand.

You shall not seek refuge
in ghosts, fortune-tellers or soothsayers.
You shall belong to no one but me.
You shall be holy. I will make you holy.
No other is your God.

When I called you from the mountain
to make you hear my words
and let you live on earth,
you came close to the foot of the mountain.
And while the mountain was burning,
the flames reaching into the very heart of the sky,
I spoke to you from the fire.
You heard the sound of words,
only a voice,
but you saw no shape.

Take care, then,
that you do not go astray,
that you do not make images of gods,
in the form of a man or a woman
or in the shape of animals, snakes, birds or fish.
Do not raise your eyes hopefully to the sky
to look out for the sun, the moon and the stars.
Do not hope for anything from that army in the heights.
Do not be subject to them,
for it is I. No other is your God.
I am the voice who brought you out
from the land of slavery,
that glowing furnace
in which you would have been melted down.

If your child asks you tomorrow
what the words that I have given you mean,
say: we were slaves in a land of darkness,
but he brought us out with his strong hand
to lead us into the land
that he promised to our fathers.
That will be a land of springs
and streams of living water,
a land full of bread, vineyards, honey and olives.
The stones there are of steel
and the mountains of copper.

We shall live there
and be satisfied.

Hear, Israel.
Heaven and earth are our witnesses
that I set before you
life and death, blessing and curse.
Choose life. Then you will live,
you and your children,
from generation to generation.

Fragments from the book of Deuteronomy

DWELL IN ME

You called us to freedom.

May we not misuse that freedom
and quite at random
each of us go his own way.

You who have spoken to us
that word that fills our souls—
be fire in us,
be good will in us,
so that we look for ways
to be able to serve each other.

May your spirit move us.
Do not let us turn away from you
and from our neighbor,
caring only for ourselves—

although we want to love,
we do not love.

Protect me from myself.
Let me not break away from you,
live uncontrolled and far beyond your reach.
Let me not worship power and money,
possessed by property,
enslaved.

Do not let us bite and tear each other.

Make us turn away from violence,
seek reconciliation,
look for friendship.
May wisdom and compassion
grow in our midst.
May peace and justice
dwell among us.

You do not dwell
in any work of human hands.
You who made us—
come now and live in us.

Dwell in me
eternally.

PRAY IN ME

1.
Loosen hope in me.
Give me the strength to keep going.
Protect me in all my ways.
Drive me and steer me,
so that I do not run aground.

Let me not conform
to the existing order
and the prevalent facts—
murder and violent death,
children maimed.

Let me not passively accept
poverty and riches.
Let me not be resigned
to injustice.
Let me not join in
the cycle of bad to worse.

Let me not—harrassed on all sides,
at my wits' end—
hand myself over to blind fate
and despair.

2.
Make me look out
for what is not yet.
Stretch me out
towards the impossible.

As a deer yearns
for living water,
make me long for the day
when we who are still divided
are assembled in your city,
united and perfected in you,
perpetuated in you.

3.
I am still in convulsions,
in the pangs of childbirth,
thinking that it will never be.

You know all my objections,
my thoughts, sick to the point of death.

You know the wrong paths
that I love to follow.

Lead me back

call me
today
by my name.

Make me remember
what you have always wanted.

Do not leave me
lost and empty,
without a future.

Put me on the right road.

4.
Make me a person
who seeks what is lost,
who is with the oppressed,
who does not run away
from another
in his misery.

Give me courage
to counterbalance
those who despair.

Let me be patient
and compassionate.
Let me be vigilant.
Pray in me.

5.
You took counsel with your heart
when you called me.
You have known me in my mother's womb.

No one will ever be strong enough
to rob me from your hand.

AGAINST MAN

We have turned against ourselves.
We have turned against man,
against the man
you saw in us.

Caught up in guilt and fear,
we blame each other.
We kill ourselves,
persisting in bitterness,
and reject our children.

Your word,
our own hearts,
the least of men—
they all accuse us.

Shall we ever be men
who no longer die?

We are yours
with all our evil.

Have mercy.

OPEN

Numbed and scornful of want
origin and aim lost
this life that is no life
still dead still unborn.
Open—you who live in light,
that we who are named after you
may not be doomed to die.

Your name in former times announced to us
persists in our ears
so that we do the fullest right
and are born of you:
"the least of men to be a neighbor"—
that word has given meaning
to our life weighed down with fear.

Those who go the ways of your word,
no other fate is granted to them
than you. You reproduce their breath,
your land will belong to them.
Deserts are drenched with dew,
happiness will befall
those who had been rejected.

AGAINST DEATH

You are the living. It is written:
men die and are not happy.

You are the living against death.
You are the most unhappy. The nearest
of all who die. You are God.

You did not, in the beginning,
want death. And since then, you fight
with the courage of despair against
our death urge, against your people's
lust to kill, against always
the same cruelty and cowardice. You are God.

You know, as no man knows, what this
unworld in like, this deathly rule
that, with its wealth and power, wisdom, violence,
leads to nothing, to no life. You know
how I am nothing, how unright, estranged
I am from myself and you. You who know
the least of men by their name, their slavery.

You who fathom their rejection. You who are
rejected in them. You saturate the ground
into which the dead are sunk
with the dew of your tears. Irreconcilable,
deadly enemy of death. You will never
bear one man to fall from you. For you are God
seeking the one who is lost.

You are: "I shall be there." It is written:
"He will wipe the traces of grief
from their faces. See, I make all things new.
You will not rest until death, that last
enemy, has fallen. Will that happen? Will you
be love then and light, gentleness, strength
in all the living, breath and heartbeat?

Who will accomplish what must be accomplished
before you are God, God in me, all in all?

WHEREVER YOU GO

Once, when they were on the way,
someone said to him:
I will follow you, wherever you go.
Jesus answered him:
the foxes have holes,
a bird has its nest,
but the son of man has nothing,
no stone to lay his head on.
To another he said:
follow me.
But the other said:
let me go home first
to bury my father.
Jesus said to him:
let the dead bury their dead,
but as for you,
follow me now
and proclaim with me
that the kingdom of God is at hand.
Another said:
I shall follow you, but first I must
take leave of my companions at home.
Jesus answered him:
whoever puts his hand to the plough,
but looks round at what is behind him
is not fit
for the kingdom of God.

Luke 9

I SHALL NOT REST

I shall not live in my house,
I shall not sleep on my bed,
I shall not close my eyes,
I shall not rest—but one moment,
until I have found
a place where he can live,
a spot where he can rest
he who is God, the only true one.

I shall not live in my house,
I shall not close my eyes,
I shall not rest—not one moment,
I may pine away with thirst
until I have found
a place where the dead live,
the spot where justice is done
to those who are rejected on earth.

HE WILL PROVIDE

Do not be troubled about your life,
about eating and drinking,
about body and clothing.
Life is more than eating and drinking,
the body is more precious than clothing.
Follow the birds in the air:
they do not sow and reap
and have no possessions in barns,
but the one who is our father in heaven
keeps them alive.

Are we not more than a few birds?
And the flowers by the wayside
that do not spin, that do not weave,
but bloom.
Solomon was dressed magnificently,
but not as beautifully as one of them.
Flowers that bloom today—
tomorrow they have gone.
But the one who is our father in heaven—
he clothes them and he cares.
Look for his kingdom and do what is right.
and he will provide.

Matthew 6

IN YOUR HAND

You who have not
written our fate in the stars,
but in your hand—
the names of all the unknown,
impenetrable, fortuitous,
eternal people that we are,
written on the palms of your hands.

You who have created us
with heart, will and understanding
and who call us
against apparent fate
by our heart, by our will,
by our name, to be destined
to die on this earth.

You who have made us,
easily broken as we are,
to be your only image—
we, strangers to each other,
widows and orphans to each other,
enemies, lovers, neighbors of each other.

You who beyond all doubt
are near and public,
in us here and now.

Direct our hearts to love and justice,
open our minds
to the vision of peace
that has called us
as long as men remember.

Fill us with the hope
that we were born
to see peace and justice
on this earth.

THE DAYS OF OUR LIFE

You who know the days of our life,
their joy, their emptiness,
their weariness.
You who are concealed
behind all death, the living,
remember us here.
You who forget no name,
despise no human child,
remember and bless us.
Do not leave this world—
we shall never be human
if you do not guide us.
Do not leave your people to each other—
Palestinians and Jews,
Zionists and Arabs,
white men and black men,
those who are hungry
and those who are full,
the poor and the rich.
You who are the origin
of all the good that is done,
be in our heart, in our soul,
in our understanding,
that we may perhaps be able
to soften the worst grief a little,
that we can outweigh the despairing,
that all those who call themselves men
do not go on destroying
this earth,
hunting and murdering men.
Make your face shine on us
and give us peace.
Remember your people
and let them not be born in vain.

EVENING PRAYER

You who have struck the night,
you who have loosened
light from the darkness,
like water from the rock,

make me rest in peace

so that I do not in the dark
imagine I am lost,
so that I do not give myself
up to dreams.

Now night has fallen on the naked—
no human hand in the world
has clothed them.
They are darkened,
your namesakes, in our midst,
the stranger, the fugitive,
children unwanted.
May a new day come
over us all.
May your kingdom come.

When over me the night has come
and I am dead, a blind spot
in the memory of those I love,
let me be secure in you
who are silence.
Do not let the second death
come over me.

NIGHT PRAYER

1.
Dust and ashes
do not glorify you.
You do not need me
to die.

2.
Heal me. Do not heal me.
What cannot be cannot be.
Heal me of my fear.

3.
There is so much I have not seen.
There are people I love.
I cannot believe it. Why
have you forsaken me?

4.
The end not yet in sight.
I see light. Feel pain.

Pain that makes me me—
I who must die
alone as we all must.

5.
Send me the angel
of ultimate comfort,
the eyes of one man.

Do not withhold from me
one man who says:
here I am.

6.
Waken gentleness in me.
Give me back
the eyes of a child.

Let me see what is.
Let me entrust myself
and not hate the light.

7.
For you are the one
greater than my heart
who saw me
before I was born.

MORNING PRAYER

Sweep away all traces of the night.
Drive death out of me.
Make me as clear
as the day that has appeared.
Let me see you,
who have appeared yourself
wrapped in the light of this day.
Make me laugh.
Raise my heart up.
Gladden me.

Make me be here.
Make me present.
Make me responsible for people.
Let me continue to be
attentive and compassionate.
Do not let me be blunted
by pain and anxiety.
May I not lose
the power to love.

Hasten the day of justice.
Do not watch any longer
while here and there in the world
people are tortured,
children are killed
and we deface the earth
and deprive each other of light.

Stir up our consciences.
Make us angry and ashamed.
Let us turn
back to your word.

MY LIFE ITSELF

You present me with life or death,
you who have called me into this life,
you who have woven me in the womb of the earth,
you who have entangled me with all that is.

You who have opened
your eyes to my eyes
and my eyes to the light.

That I should live in your light
and see people—
that is your will.
You want me to belong
to people, not to be elusive,
inaccessible, closed, aimless, dead,
a victim of illusion.

That I should choose life—that is your will;
that I should do justice to my neighbors
and respond to those I love.
That is the life
that you have set before men's eyes,
for which you made him and inspired him.

Inspire me with your will.
Breathe me open.

Enlighten my heart.
Dwell in my conscience.

May I not curse
my destiny, my birth.
May I experience
the blessing of your word.

May I understand your name
and cling to you
who are not a god of the dead,
but the God
of all the living.

You are
my life itself
in good and in evil days.

ISRAEL

Other gods, not you,
have ruled over me.
People, their mouths full of words,
have hunted me down.
No one has comforted me.
No one has seen my tears.

You, however, consoled me,
but did not spare me.
You fought with me,
you wounded me,
blessed me and emptied me,
but still I am not dead.

Shivering with desire
I go, for ever awakened,
into the cold of the morning
as far as you want to lead me.
I walk with a limp for ever,
but I go in a new name.

For Abel Herzberg

THE GREAT LITANY

Be here among us, light in the midst of us.
Show your glory for us to see.
Stir up your power and liberate us.

Be here among us, word given to us.
Be here among us, flame of our life.
Flame of our life, meaning of life.
Liberate us, God of our life.

Your rescue dawns like the light in the morning.
Come and appear, be light to our eyes.

God of our life, let us hear you,
let us know you with heart and soul.
Living God, not a god of the dead,
may we know you—bring us to life.
Or are you, God, no god of people?
Be here among us, bring us to life.

For you are God, light in the morning.
You are the only one, today and tomorrow.
Since living memory you are God.
Holy, eternal, a God of people.
Soul of our heart, light of our light,
a God so far and yet so near.

Nobody has ever seen you,
except your son, the son of people.
Only your son is our guide.
Jesus messiah, flame of our life.
Word given to us, light in the midst of us,
born in us, God in our midst.

Living dead one, living love.
Holy God, immortal God.
Be here among us, do not let us fall.
Do not let us fall back into the dust.
See us, tolerate us, be gracious to us.
Be gracious, do not let us die.

May we not live imprisoned in emptiness.
May we not go on ways that lead nowhere.
What is the earth if you do not exist?
Send us your spirit and we are recreated.
Be our breath, be in our blood.
Breathe us open and we shall not die.

Call us by name, living love.
Living God, why must we die?
For not the dead will speak of you,
for not the dead in their silence.
But we, the living, on this night,
call out your name and want to see you.

We exist through you, we exist in you.
You exist in our restless calling.
We who wander in this night
thirst for you, source of our life.
All the living thirst for you.
Open yourself and we shall be filled.

Tear the clouds apart and come.
Here and now—be our God. Who else?
No one else has ever called us
as a loved one: "Open me, eat me."
"Here I am," you have called.
"Drink my soul, divide me, here I am."

No one else has ever called so.
And the depths have heard it.
Where are you now? Where was your passion?
Are you no longer the one that you were?
O come back, restore us to honor,
word given to us, once and for all.

With all your people, all over the world,
we call to you on this night.
In this city, this house full of people,
here in this body, be our peace.
In these days, be our peace.
On our tables, the bread of peace.

For our children, peace at last.
No one rejected, no child lost.
O God, come back, your will be done.
Your name be hallowed, your new earth.
How long must we go on waiting for you,
people for people, all things for all men?

We place our trust in you, living God,
and would you ever put that trust to shame?

ALIVE AGAIN

I was touched by his hand,
I was led by his spirit
into the middle of the valley,
the valley of death, full of bones.

He asked me: son of man,
will these dry bones
ever live again?
I replied: You know.

He said:
Call to these bones and say:
dry bones,
listen to the word
of him who is and was
and who will be, he says:
I shall put a spirit into you,
so that you will live again.
I shall cover you with sinews
and make flesh grow over you.
I shall draw a skin over you
and blow the breath of life into you,
so that you will live again.

And you will know
that I am for you.

And while I was doing
what I had been told,
I heard a sound.
The bones were moving
towards each other
and were covered with sinews and flesh
and a skin was drawn over them.
But they were still dead.

Then he said to me:
Call for the spirit and say:
he who is and was
and who will be says:
Come, spirit,
from the four corners of the earth
and blow into these dead men,
so that they will live again.

I did as I had been told
and the spirit came
into the dry bones
and they lived again
and stood up—
so many that no one could count them.

Then he said to me:
Son of man,
these bones are my people.
They are sighing:
"We are dry and dead
and our hope has vanished."
Now you must say to them:
he who is and was
and who will be says:

I shall open your graves
and raise you from your graves,
O my people,
and lead you back
to your native soil.
And when I have opened your graves
and have raised you from your graves,
O my people,
I shall pour my breath into you
and you will know
that I am for you.

A vision of the prophet Ezechiel

HOLY SPIRIT

When the day had come
they were all under one roof.

Suddenly out of the sky there came
a violent sound, as though from the wind
that rises and comes
in fits and starts.
And the whole of their house
was full of that voice.

Fire appeared, in tongues
descending on every head.

They were filled with breath and strength
and spoke in foreign languages.

And all who had gathered together
in that town
heard them and understood

their mother's language
their father's name

the call of today
and of yesterday and for ever

the voice of their heart
their mind and their soul

the living word
the cry of birth and death
the cry of people.

REVEALED

He who is our God and father—
may he keep us and make us grow
in love for each other and all men
until everything is revealed in his light.
He will make us holy and strengthen our hearts
and we shall stand before him blameless
on that day that Jesus our lord will come
and everything is revealed in his light.

According to 1 Thessalonians 3:12

OUR FATHER

1.
Our father, source of our life,
heart that wanted us, voice that calls us:
you are in secret, in night and clouds,
in light that blinds our eyes, not here.
Not in words. You do not dwell in images.
Not in all things. In all beauty
we know you, but do not touch you.
Never can you be embraced or kissed—
you are no hand in our hand, no shoulder.
From afar we greet you, distance itself.

2.
Only your name is here, entrusted
to our memory, sowed in our soul
like storm and peace, called out
in the empty space of our conscience. Ever,
when you thought of us and loved us, when you
turned us towards you. A strange old sore,
suspicion of happiness, understanding of justice,
hope that cannot be destroyed—that is your name
in us. Just as no sea can penetrate
the hardest stone, so you have penetrated people with
     you.

3.
May your name be named, be known and loved,
fulfilled, made holy. By us, doing right,
establishing justice. The soil of the earth,
the constellations will belong
to those who now are still rejected.
The light will be given back to the blind.

The poor and the downtrodden, risen
from their doom and damnation, those who have been
dispossessed and dead, submissive to ghosts,
carry their right in their own hands and live.

4.

It must be so, may your kingdom come.
The old made new, the whites scrubbed clean,
the blacks made blacker. Peace and justice
like suns in the sky. People, good, bad,
hard, dear, enslaved, silenced, torn to shreds,
will be healed and reconciled, one new
eternal man. All of us. And I too,
grown into what I was destined to be, veined through
shown through and through with your word.
And no more whispering of lies.
And nothing more that cannot be spoken.

5.

The earth will be heaven. And there will be
no longer night. Made open to each other,
we live in names sparkling translucent,
live beside luminous water branching wide,
breathe and are in you. City of crystal.
Then I will be like you. As one
chance man happens to be like another: eyes
see seas purple; feet, tired with walking,
rest; and lips, hard from too many words,
relax. And the silence lasts and lasts.

6.

Why do you not hasten the time? How long
will these remain unfulfilled words
and shall we be made ridiculous with such a vision,
dreamers who cannot get accustomed to facts?
O your will certainly will be done, ever,
but not on earth, in this vale of hunger.

Give us today our bread, we tell you,
and there is bread, but just farther on
there is no bread for such people as us.
Why are you not a God of all people?

7.
You are the God who is as much as people
can be for each other, bread, love and peace.
You are unthinkably more than we can do
here to each other. You are powerless
in my hands, like the least of men; my child,
defenseless, looking, waiting, crying for love—
that is how you are God for me, not otherwise.
The only one whom I have then and then
done wrong. Who alone can forgive me.
Forgive me seventy times a thousand times.

8.
Forgive those who do not know what they do,
who live and die in blindness,
like storms of violence, gusts of hate,
who cry with disasters, cursing
the day that they were born, imploring
darkness, that it may cover them, despairing,
driving your word out of their heart. O you
who know everything, be greater than their heart.
Curtail their suffering. Implore them to you.
Be God and clothe with light what you have made.

9.
How long will violence in word and weapon
fill the air? But the poor man, groaning,
is not heard. And truth like a lamb
is silent before his slaughterer. And the gods sing.
But even before they have taken out
their black score they will be dead and silent.
The song of life of the poor does not die out.

You have chosen the least of all,
the despised. Singing you will harvest
what you have sown in tears.

10.
The donkey knows the manger of his lord,
the ox knows his man—may we know you.
You are the eyes that see us from afar,
hand that made us from clay and breath.
You can complete us too. You are God.
Climbing sun, light that charges us with light,
love that arouses love, fire that purifies
until we are people. Make us know you
lead us past death. Voice that calls us.
Source. Heart. Beginning and end. Our father.

LOVE

If I speak with tongues
of angels and men,
but have no love,
I am ringing copper,
a tinkling tambourine.
I may be a prophet,
seeing what cannot be seen,
initiated into everything,
my faith may be so perfect
that I can move mountains,
but if I have no love
I am nothing.

If I give everything away
and let myself be tortured
if I have to,
but have no love,
then it is useless.
Love is giving space,
leaving time, goodness, patience.
Love is not petty minded,
jealous, grasping.
Love does not assert itself,
is not vain, coarse, unapproachable.
Whoever loves
does not concentrate on himself.
Love is not bitter.
Love is not unforgiving.
Injustice makes love unhappy,
truth makes it happy.
Love stands firm against everything.
It believes again and again.
It endures all things,
is again and again filled with hope.
Love never breaks down.
Prophetic words fail
and languages are silent.
All knowledge is finite.
All that we know is piece-work
and our visions are shreds of light.
But when the infinite dawns,
all that is finite will cease.

When I was a little child,
I talked as children do
and thought no further
than children do.
Now that I have become a man,
I have left all that behind.
Now we still see in mirror-images,
mysteriously,
but then we shall be eye to eye.
Now I only half know,
but some time I shall know all things,
as he knows about me.
Faith and hope and love
will remain, all three,
but the greatest is love.

1 Corinthians 13

MAN

As on the mountains the storm falls into the oak trees,
so the passion of love fell on to me and passed through
    me,
says Sappho.

So too the vision of man in his splendor
falls on to me and passes through me. The man
who I shall be. The man in us all. Who still
scarcely, still unnamed, grows in this poor body
that rages like pain in us, like a child that
kicks and turns round in the womb of its mother.

CITY OF CRYSTAL

And I saw a new heaven
a new earth.

And I saw the city of peace,
descending from heaven, from God—
a city clothed with pure light,
sparkling like the most precious stone
flashing like crystal,
with gates made of pearls.
And the streets of that city
were of pure gold,
transparent as glass.
And a river of living water,
clear as crystal,
flowed through that city
and on its banks stood
the trees of life.

And I heard calling
a powerful voice;
This is the house of God,
here he will live with his people,
he who wants to be their God.
He will wipe all tears from their eyes
and death will be no more,
no sighing and groaning,
no pain and no sorrow will be
and night will also be no more.

And the one on the throne said:
I make all things new.

From the book of Revelation 21-22

FOR PEACE

Much too late I learned to love you
beauty how old you are how new you are
much too late I learned to love you.
You were within me, I was outside
and I sought you as a blind man seeing
outside myself and, poured out like water,
I ran away from you and I was lost
amid so much beauty, but it was not you.
Then you called and cried aloud to me,
breaking through the barrier of my deafness.
You appeared in light that blinded me
because you wanted to put my blindness to flight.
You shed fragrance and I breathed it in,
I still gasp for breath and long for you.
I tasted you and since that time am thirsty
and hunger for you. Easily touched,
I was set alight by you. And now I
burn and blaze towards you—for peace.

From Augustine's Confessions 10:27

114